CANTABILE

Duets for Mandolin and Guitar

by Butch Baldassari and John Mock

www.melbay.com/95734EB

Guitar

1 2 3 4 5 6 7 8 9 0

Visit us on the Web at www.melbay.com — E-mail us at email@melbay.com

Table of Contents

The Quadro Pavin

Richard Allison
arranged by John Mock

Galliard to the Quadro Pavin

Richard Allison
arranged by John Mock

La Coranto

I

Thomas Morley
arranged by John Mock

13
p
17
21

Phillips Pavin

Phillips
arranged by John Mock

Galliard to the Phillips Pavin

Phillips
arranged by John Mock

This page has been left blank
to avoid awkward page turns.

Arioso

J. S. Bach
arranged by John Mock

Jesu, Joy of Man's Desiring

J. S. Bach
arranged by John Mock

1/2 III
1/2 V
VIII
1/2 V
VII

Menuets I & II

G. F. Handel
arranged by John Mock

D. C.

Sonata #483

Domenico Scarlatti
arranged by John Mock

41
4
1
0
1.
2.
45
mf
f
52
p
59
mf
p
65
f
p
71
f
77
ff

Sonatine

Ludwig van Beethoven
arranged by John Mock

Adagio

29
32
37
41

Cantabile

Niccolo Paganini
arranged by John Mock

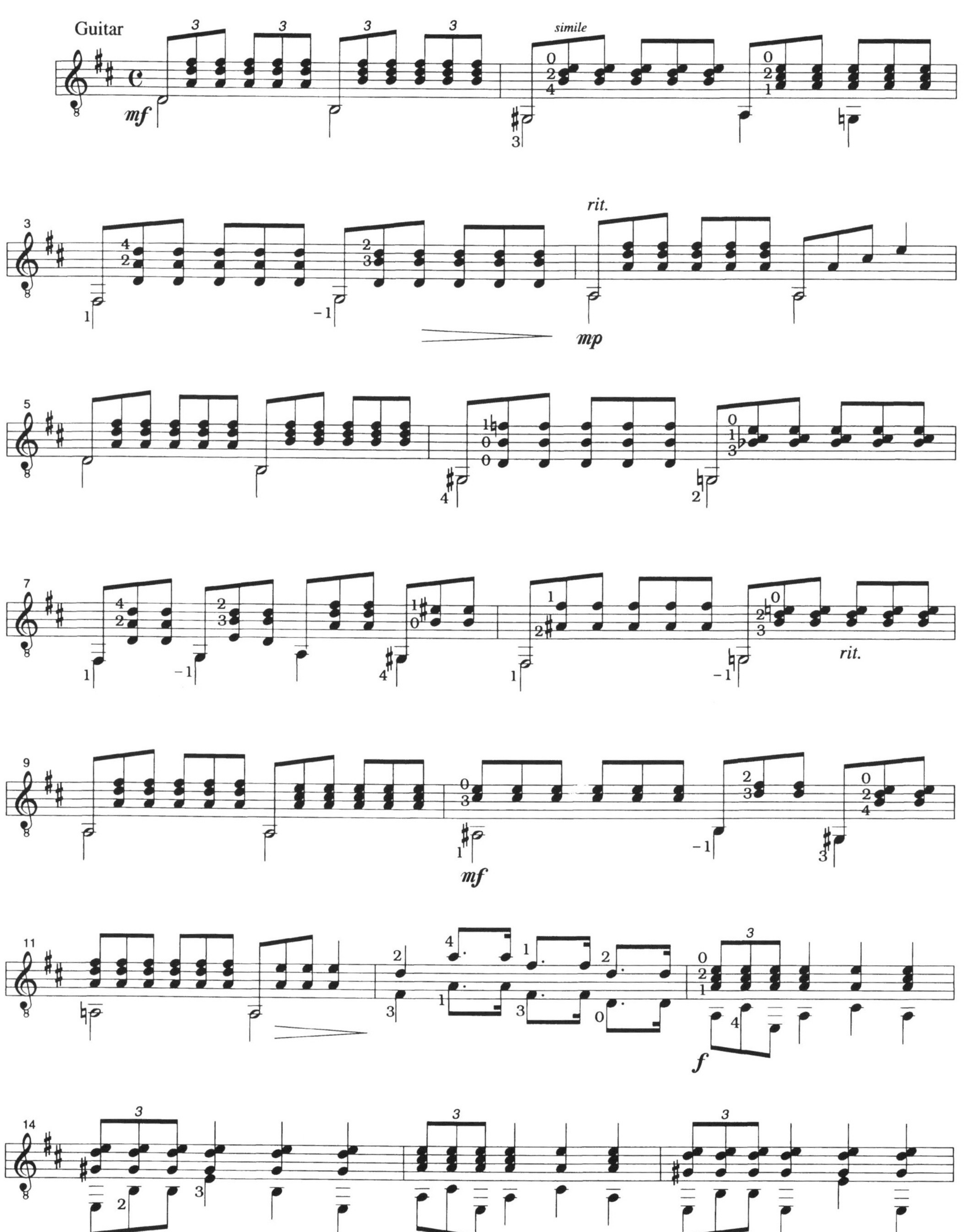

CI
mp
mf
sub mp
CII
rit.
f

p
ff
rit.
rit.
rit.
CI
rit.
p
morendo

Estudio #6

Fernando Sor
arranged by John Mock

Recuerdos de la Alhambra

Francisco Tárrega
arranged by John Mock

31
35
Last time to Coda
1.
39
2.
D.S. al Coda
(without repeats)
43
47
51
55
59

Gymnopedie #1

Eric Satie
arranged by John Mock

38
4
1
0
0
44
44
50
56
60
62
68
74

This page has been left blank
to avoid awkward page turns.

Bolero

Calace
arranged by John Mock

cantabile
pp

III
p

Romance

Ludwig van Beethoven
arranged by John Mock

CANTABILE

Duets for Mandolin and Guitar

by Butch Baldassari and John Mock

Mandolin

1 2 3 4 5 6 7 8 9 0

Visit us on the Web at www.melbay.com — E-mail us at email@melbay.com

Table of Contents

The Quadro Pavin

Richard Allison
arranged by John Mock

Galliard to the Quadro Pavin

La Coranto

Thomas Morley
arranged by John Mock

I

Phillips Pavin

Phillips
arranged by John Mock

Galliard to the Phillips Pavin

Arioso

J. S. Bach
arranged by John Mock

Jesu, Joy of Man's Desiring

J. S. Bach
arranged by John Mock

Menuets I & II

G. F. Handel
arranged by John Mock

18
24
1 4 3 2 1
30
36
42
48
tr
D. C.

Sonata #483

Domenico Scarlatti
arranged by John Mock

1.
2.
mp
mf
f
mf
p
mf
f
p
f
ff
f

Sonatine

Ludwig van Beethoven
arranged by John Mock

28
3
1
3
1
4
4
2
1
3
1
4
2
1
2
1

32
trem.
0
1
1
2
2
1
3
2
1
1
2
p
mf

37
1
2
1
2
1
1
trem.
3
2
1
1
3
1

42
1
3
2
p
1
1
2
3
4
4
3
harm.

Cantabile

Niccolo Paganini
arranged by John Mock

rit.
mp
rit.
rit.
f
p
ff
free rhythm
p
dolce
mf
rit.
free rhythm
p

Romance

Ludwig van Beethoven
arranged by John Mock

Estudio #6

Fernando Sor
arranged by John Mock

Recuerdos de la Alhambra

Francisco Tárrega
arranged by John Mock

Gymnopedie #1

Eric Satie
arranged by John Mock

Bolero

Calace
arranged by John Mock

appass.
ten.
a tempo
allarg. ff
appass.

affrett.
dim.
affrett.
dim.
ten.
a tempo
ff
cresc.
risol.
ff

CANTABILE

Duets for Mandolin and Guitar

by Butch Baldassari and John Mock

Score

1 2 3 4 5 6 7 8 9 0

Visit us on the Web at www.melbay.com — E-mail us at email@melbay.com

Table of Contents

The Quadro Pavin

Richard Allison
arranged by John Mock

Galliard to the Quadro Pavin

Mandolin

4

Guitar

7

4

13

19

mf

La Coranto

I

Thomas Morley
arranged by John Mock

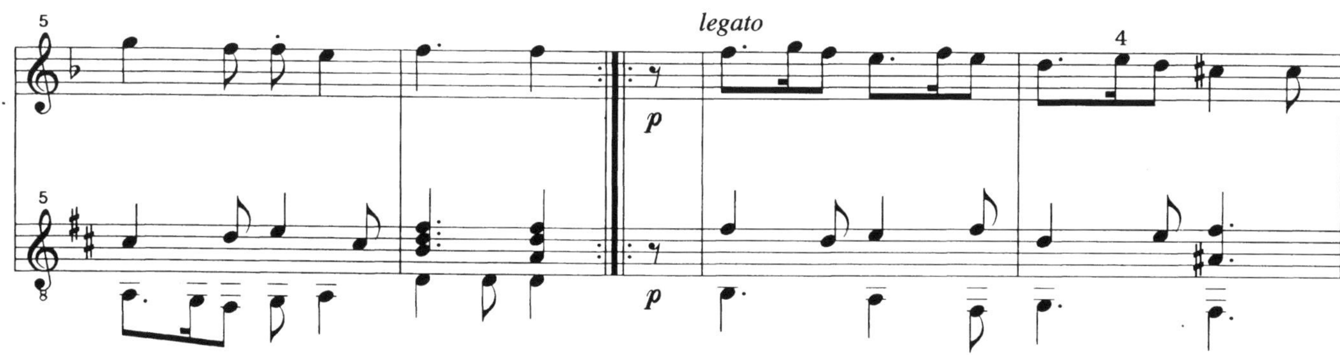

II

5
9
13
legato
p
4
17
tr
21

Phillips Pavin

Phillips
arranged by John Mock

Galliard to the Phillips Pavin

Phillips
arranged by John Mock

Jesu, Joy of Man's Desiring

J. S. Bach
arranged by John Mock

Menuets I & II

G. F. Handel
arranged by John Mock

II

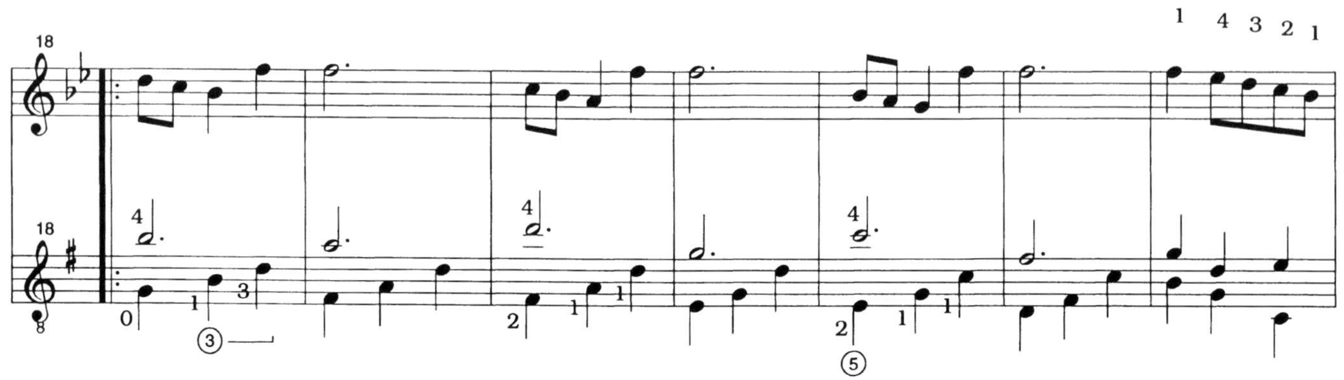

25
25
32
32
39
39
45
45
tr
D. C.
D. C.

Arioso

J. S. Bach
arranged by John Mock

20
tr
VI
III
25
29
p
34
tr

Romance

Ludwig van Beethoven
arranged by John Mock

Sonata #483

Domenico Scarlatti
arranged by John Mock

1.
2.

Sonatine

Ludwig van Beethoven
arranged by John Mock

trem.
trem.
harm.

Cantabile

Niccolo Paganini
arranged by John Mock

mf
mf
rit.
f
f
CI

rit.
8va
tr
sub mp
rit.
CII
rit.
mp
mf
rit.
rit.

CII
free rhythm
rit.

39
dolce
rit.
41
43
rit.
mf
CI
45
rit.
free rhythm
46
p
morendo

This page has been left blank
to avoid awkward page turns.

Estudio #6

Fernando Sor
arranged by John Mock

17
17
0
21
2
4
3
0
3
4
2
21
25
25
29
4
29

Recuerdos de la Alhambra

Francisco Tárrega
arranged by John Mock

Last time to Coda
1.
2.
D.S. al Coda
(without repeats)
mp
mf
pp
ppp
harm. 12

Gymnopedie #1

Eric Satie
arranged by John Mock

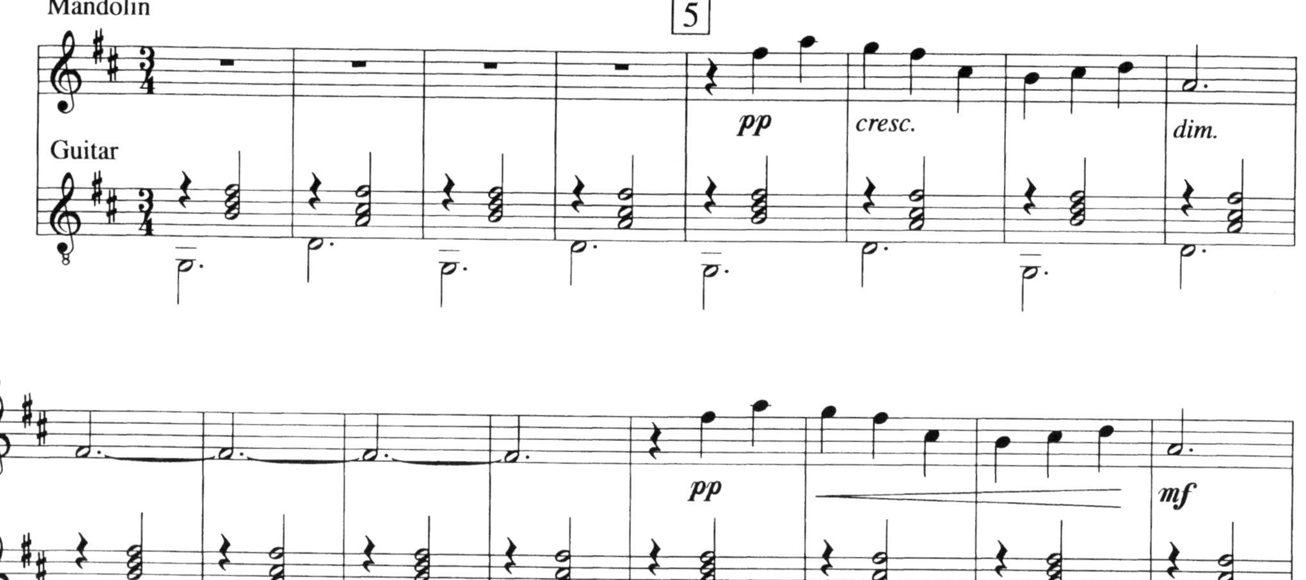

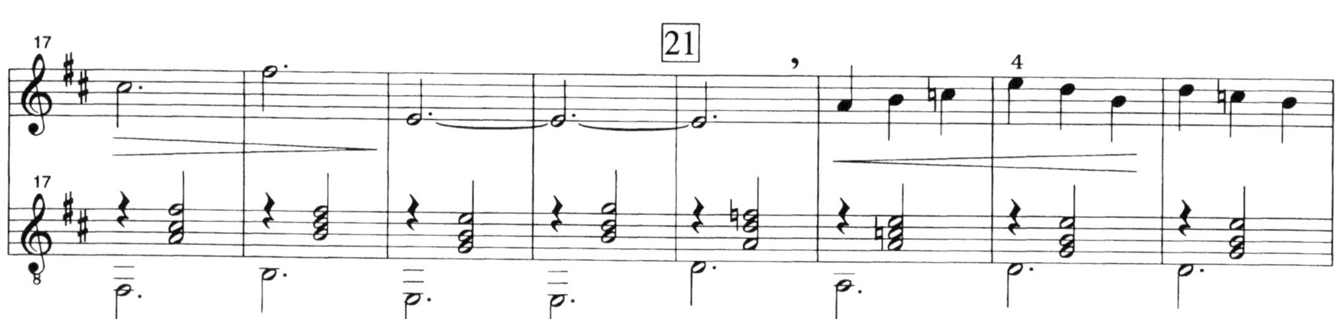

44
pp
cresc.
dim.
pp
60
f
p

Bolero

Calace
arranged by John Mock

dim.
rall.
rall.
appass.
cantabile
ten.
a tempo

allarg. ff
pp
appass.
affrett.
dim.
affrett.

dim.
ten.
a tempo
III
p
ff
cresc.
risol.
ff

Butch Baldassari

Mandolinist Butch Baldassari has created new interest in this age-old instrument and is luring legions of new admirers to the music he creates.

With mastery of a wide variety of mandolin styles, Baldassari's versatility is unmatched. he moves from bluegrass festivals to symphony halls with ease and grace, earning respect and admiration in these seemingly disparate worlds.

Not just a performer and bandleader, Baldassari is widely respected as a teacher, currently serving as Adjunct Associate Professor of Mandolin at Vanderbilt University's renowned Blair School of Music. His instructional videos, books and tapes are among the most widely used by aspiring mandolin players, and his workshops at festivals including *Telluride, Rocky Grass Bluegrass Academy, Winterhawk* and *Grass Valley* are standing-room-only sessions. His annual appearances at the *Classical Mandolin Society* are among the event's most popular.

With his own successful record label, SoundArt Recordings, Baldassari has broadened both his reach to new audiences, and his influence on the music.

In Butch Baldassari and the music he creates, the past, present and future of this small, yet richly powerful instrument are in the best of hands.

www.soundartrecordings.com
email: info@soundartrecordings.com

John Mock

Multi-instrumentalist John Mock has recorded/performed with such notable artists as The Dixie Chicks, James Taylor, Nanci Griffith, Mark O'Connell, Rosanne Cash, Kathy Mattea, Sylvia, Mark O'Connor, Michael Johnson and Melissa Manchester.

His talents in string arranging and orchestration have placed him at the heart of many Nashville projects. He has also written a number of symphonic arrangements for Nanci Griffith which appear on her Elektra CD release: *Dust Bowl Symphony,* recorded in England with the London Symphony Orchestra.

In 1995 he furthered his knowledge and passion of celtic music by joining the traditional group Isla, playing pennywhistles, bodhran, concertina and mandolin.

As a composer, John has recorded two solo CD releases: *New England Portraits* and *Celtic Portraits* for Green Hill records in Nashville, TN. He has also composed commissioned works for the Nashville Chamber Orchestra.

John is featured here as an arranger and guitarist.